Giant African La

Giant African Land Snails as pets.

Giant African Land Snail Complete Care Guide

By

Joseph Dunbury

Table of Contents

Introduction

This book has been put together as a general and pocket size guide to the care of Giant African Land Snails or "GALS" as they are known to the owners and breeders. As a "GALS" owner I often found the information conflicting in regards to feeding, housing and general health care of the snail so after speaking with a fellow "GALS" owner we have decided to put this short but informative guide together to help new and existing owners on the basics including housing, breeding, feeding and health care. We certainly are no experts but below is what we do which works well for our snails. You will find the guide split into easy to read sections with a final page of links to further information.

What are Giant African Land Snails?

Giant African Land Snails are gastropods or "belly footers" to some people. They are native to western and eastern Africa but have become a favorite household pet for families and individuals in the UK. They can grow between 7 and 10 inches depending on species and breed, and their shells usually reach heights of 2 inches but again will be dependent on breed/size. The "GALS" are often referred to as a vegetarian, but they are herbivores, while it's true that they will happily eat vegetarian you can also feed your snail raw minced beef and dog feed as treats.

The snails themselves are hermaphrodites, which plainly means they possess both male and female reproductive parts and are capable of producing both sperm and ova. Life expectancy of these creatures is usually between 5 and 7 years in captivity but in the right conditions and with the correct care could live up to 10 years old. They are most active at night and in the early evening but will happily crawl around eating and showing off during the day if their care is correct. This guide is strictly for use within the United Kingdom and Ireland as current laws forbid the keeping of "GALS" in countries such as America and Canada.

They inhabit nearly all ecosystems in the world, in both aquatic and terrestrial environments. Perhaps the best known, and arguably fascinating mollusks, are the Gastropoda, or slugs and snails. Snails are probably most recognized for their shells, which appear in a myriad of different forms, colors, and sizes. The smallest currently known species is Angustopila Dominika with a tank length of just 0.86mm (0.03in). (Although new research suggests that record may soon be beaten with an even smaller species)! With a total length up to 39.3 cm (15.5in), the largest terrestrial species is Achatina cheating, commonly known as the Giant Ghanaian or Giant African Land Snail (Guinness World Records 2016). Giant African Land Snails (Achatinidae) belong to a family of medium to large sized terrestrial tropical mollusks. The name "Achatinidae" is from "Achates," the Greek for agate: a brightly colored layered rock. They are all native to sub-Saharan Africa, although they have been introduced to many other areas.

One of the most commonly kept species of Giant African Land Snail is the Giant East African Snail (Achatina Fulica). Other popular species include the Giant Ghana Snail or Tiger Snail (Achatina cheating), the Giant West African Snail (Archachatina marginal) and the Giant Zanzibar Snail (Achatina Zanzibar ice). Where they are legal to keep, they should never be released into the wild due to the potential damage they can cause to native ecosystems.

Giant African Land Snails can make beautiful, entertaining and educational pets for people of all ages. They are an excellent choice as a first pet for children or classroom pets due to their slow rate of movement (the average speed for a Giant African Land Snail is about 0.04 miles per hour) and relatively low maintenance. They can also be observed and studied safely without the need for frequent handling and so offer an excellent introduction for younger children into the captivating world of nature.

Chapter 1: An overview of the African Land Snail

1. What is a snail?

The snail is a terrestrial shell-bearing animal of approximately 100,000 species of the Phylum Mollusca, or alternately any of the twelve species of land pulmonate gastropods used as human food. It is air breathing, usually herbivorous, with a complex hermaphrodite reproductive system though demanding cross-fertilization. It usually hibernates, forming a membrane over the shell opening known as Aestivation. Snail Rearing is called heliculture.

2. Snail rearing

Breeding of edible land snails began in Nigeria in the early 1980's with interest increasing by the day as production is found to be viable and profitable. There are several types of snails in Nigeria and selection of the species to rear depends on the need of the consumer. However, the most commonly available ones are:

- The African giant snail or big black snail Archachatina marginata. Most common in Nigeria with high value.
- Archatina achatina: Very attractive also and has distinct black stripes with a brown background. The foot is usually grey.

- Archatina fulica: (Akikor) the garden snail. Small but multiplies and grows very fast. Can also withstand harsh environmental conditions.
- Archachatine degneris: This is found mainly in the savannah areas. It has a bitter taste because of the neem leaves it eats making it unacceptable to many consumers.
- Limicolaria sp.: Has a smallish and narrow shell.

For the purpose of rearing for profit and household consumption, the Africa giant snail – Archachatina marginata should be considered because of its size. A mature snail of this type weighs between 400 – 800g with a shell length of between 15 – 17cm. Young ones from this species, having five complete whorls of the tank, without broken shells or deformities should be selected for breeding. They can begin to lay eggs within a year. The eggs are laid in holes 2 – 5cm deep in the soil or on the surface. Those on the surface should be covered with soil properly. The snail eggs, which should be watered daily, hatch in 24 – 35days. And they should be watered until hatching. Cold weather delays during warm weather accelerates hatching.

Snails attain old age at 24 – 30 months and starts laying eggs at 9 – 10 months. Snails prefer a damp and shady habitat. Snail's egg laying ability depends on the species, which ranges between 20 – 170 eggs each growing season. Though snails are hermaphrodite, they practice sexual reproduction.

At least three snails should be kept in a pen so that mating can take place.

You may have noticed that plant and animal species are given a common name and a scientific name. For example, the Giant West African Snail, has the common name, 'Giant West African Snail' as well as the scientific name 'Archachatina marginata'. But having two names seems overly complicated, so why is this?

In theory, every known species on Earth is given a double-barreled scientific name, that is unique to that particular species, whereas common names can vary from country to country and even by regions within a country.

This system works because there are sets of universal rules about how to name species and zoologists try to avoid calling the same thing more than once (though this does sometimes happen).

Let's take us Humans as a pretty well-known example: our binomial name is Homo sapiens, the generic designation is Homo, and the specific epithet is sapiens. The general designation is the name of the genus (singular form of general) to which we belong, the genus Homo. The binomial naming system (in its current form) dates back as far as the 1700's! Although primarily developed by the Swiss Bauhin brothers, Gaspard and Johann, 200 years earlier, the botanist and physician Carl Linnaeus (1707–1778) is regarded as its creator.

They may relate to the individual scientist that was involved in discovering them or connect to the native language of where they are found, or to the regions where the species is found, they also may refer to some physical or behavioral trait of the species. Scientific names are also designed to tell you something about the animal's relationships with other animals.

To avoid confusion I should state that in this book (well from now on) when we first use a binomial name we will use the complete name, i.e. Achatina Fulica, while after that we will shorten it to A. This is not a new species but just a shorthand way of writing their name.

3. Do Giant African Land Snails Make Good Pets?

Different species need to be kept at different temperatures. The most common Giant African Land Snail species found in pet shops, need to be maintained at around 20 °C – 28 °C and not exceeding 29 °C. If the temperature is 2 °C – 10 °C then this species is likely to go into hibernation.

But don't be fooled! Giant land snails still need regular, quality care and require commitment – after all many exceed ten years of age. An adult should always be responsible for checking that any child's pet is being adequately cared for. What Will I Need to Have A Giant Land Snail?

To successfully keep a giant land snail, there are some things which you need to have, as well as some stuff that you should have thought about.

You will need:

- A vivarium or tank
- A calcium supply – cuttlefish bones, or egg shells
- Substrate
- Giant land snail food
- A heat mat

You will also have needed to think about:

- How many snails you'll be getting
- What you'll do with the babies, if the snails breed (which is likely)
- Who will look after them when you're on holiday

It is illegal to only release giant land snails into the wild as they are invasive species.

It is also illegal to keep giant land snails as pets in some countries, so check before you buy!

How Many Snails Should I Get?

Typically, people who have giant land snails keep two or three in the same tank. However, as snails are hermaphrodites, any pair of snails will breed. (And in sporadic cases a snail can reproduce by himself).

So, if you plan on keeping more than one snail, you will need to decide what you will be doing with the babies. You can either let them hatch, and sell them, or humanely dispose of the eggs. Never release them into the wild (it is illegal to do this), and never eat any snails or eggs, as some species have been thought to carry salmonella in rare cases.

4. Description

In the wild, Achatinidae are nocturnal forest dwellers. As a prey species, concealed habitats, such as deep leaf litter, are preferred. In general, Achatinidae become more active during periods of high humidity, for example after heavy rainfall.

The Achatinidae is a large family including some 13 genera (depending on which taxonomist you are talking to). Of these, four species are commonly kept as pets; A. cheating, A. Julia, A. marginal and A. Zanzibar ice. All seem superficially similar, but significant differences do exist.

Achatina Fulica A. Julia, also known as Lissachatina Julia, has a narrower more conical shell that is roughly twice as long as it is wide and contains 7-9 whorls when fully grown. Adults of the species may exceed 20cm (7.8in) in shell length but average about 5 to 10cm (2 to 4in). Four subspecies are currently designated for A. flick, with distinct populations and characteristics; A. Julia Camilleri, A. fulica Ro DAT Zi, A. fulica sinistrosa and A. fulica umbilicata. Selective breeding has also produced a range of different color morphs of this species, the naming of which can be inconsistent between breeders so it can get confusing.

Archachatina marginata: A. marginata can grow up to approximately 21cm (8.3in) in length and 13cm (5.1in) in diameter, although a smaller size is more typical. In the wild A. marginata seem to appear more variable in its physical characteristics than other species, the body color, for example, can be relatively variable; albino or tan to ash grey colored individuals being encountered commonly. In the past partially striped or elongated shelled specimens in captivity were sold as Achatina smithii, but these are now generally thought of as a type of A. marginata.

Achatina zanzibarica: A. zanzibarica is medium-sized and rather thinner and lighter than the other species, being 8 to 13.5cm (3.1 to 5.3in) long when fully grown, with 6.5-7.5 whorls in its shell. Achatina zanzibarica is notable for being one of the few Achatinidae that are truly ovoviviparous; meaning they can produce live offspring rather than laying eggs externally.

It is true for snails as it is for other group and there are now a unique species of snail appearing for sale. Some rare or less commonly kept species of Achatinidae include:

Achatina craveni: A. craveni, sometimes known as the Zebra Snail due to its colouration, is a very rarely kept species. In the wild, they live in Southern Africa at high altitudes, approximately 1300 meters above sea level. Hatchling snails are tiny, only 2mm (0.07in.) in shell length, with adult snails only growing to around 5cm (1.9in.). Interestingly these snails seem to cause a significant amount of damage to coffee plantations in their natural range - perhaps they need the caffeine hit!

Achatina iredalei: A. iredalei only grows to about 7cm (2.7in.) shell length in total. The snails in captivity can have either light or dark body colors. Snails with a light body color are much more commonly seen. Shell color ranges from a light cream to yellow. This species is found in coastal woodland, on sandy ground.

Achatina reticulata: A. reticulata is one of the larger Achatinidae species; they can grow to around 21cm (8.2in.) in shell length, though in captivity shells of around 12-16cm (4.7-6.2in.) are more likely for adult snails. Their shells are very slender for their size. These were once very rare in captivity but are becoming more common due to success in captive breeding.

5. Snails as Food

During the war, as a young girl, my Nan was sent out with a bucket on rainy mornings to collect 'wall fruit' to supplement their food ration. 'Wall fruit' was in fact Garden Snails (Cornu asper sum or Helix aspersa)! To many people, the eating of snails is considered pretty revolting, but roasted snail shells have been found in archaeological excavations, an indication that man has eaten snails since prehistoric times.

Heliciculture is the name given to the process of farming or raising snails for food. For many people worldwide, in particular West and Central Africa and the Tropics, heliciculture and the collecting of wild snails provide a valuable source of cheap, readily available protein. In certain rural locations in Cameroon and Ghana sales of

16

snail meat accounted for between 42% and 62% of a community's income, suggesting snails can play a significant role in potentially reducing poverty and theoretically producing sustainable foodstuff. Unfortunately, over-harvesting from the wild has caused populations to plummet in some of the snail's natural range. As they are relatively simple to raise successfully in captivity, and as research grows in this area, hopefully, farmed snails will help meet demand and give wild stock levels a chance to recover.

This book is designed for the keeper of snails as pets, not as a guide to heliciculture (perhaps I'll save that for another book) and I probably wouldn't recommend eating your pet snails! That said, if the need does become apparent, I can only suggest you don't name them first and that you cook them very well!

6. Invasive Status

Several Achatinidae species have been accidentally or purposefully transported to areas outside their native range in Africa where they have become a serious pest, the most notable of which being A. fulica - this species is listed as one of the top 100 invasive species in the world!

Giant African Land Snails can cause significant ecological and economic damage in these new areas. A. fulica cause extensive damage to a large number of plants in tropical and sub-tropical agriculture, examples of which can be seen in Figure 5. They also cause further problems for farmers by spreading plant diseases.

Examples of commercial plant species recorded as being damaged by A. fulica

Common Name	Binomial Name
Banana	Musa acuminata
Beans	Arachis hypogaea
Carrot	Daucus carota
Figs	Ficus hispida
Lettuce	Lactuca sativa
Papaya	Carica papaya
Peas	Pisum sativum
Tea	Camellia sinensis
Tobacco	Nicotiana tabacum
Tomato	Lycopersicon esculentum

The introduction of Achatinidae to new areas also has directly or indirectly caused the extinctions of some indigenous species. People have tried to control these invasive populations through a variety of means, from physically collecting them to chemical and biological control methods. In Florida, they even have specially-trained dogs to sniff out the snails!

Interestingly, some of the biological controls meant to reduce Achatinidae numbers have caused more damage to native snail populations, even causing species extinctions. For instance, the carnivorous Euglandina rose or Cannibal Snail native to Central America was introduced to Hawaii and other Pacific Islands to try and control numbers of A. fulica. Unfortunately, the Cannibal Snail preferred the taste of the native O'ahu Tree Snails (Achatinella sp.) and Polynesian Tree Snails (Partula sp.) causing numerous species extinctions within the first few years. To add insult to injury, the introduction of E. rose seems to have no effect on the spread of A. fulica. Unfortunately, E. rose is still used by some government agencies despite warnings from qualified scientists that the effects could be ecologically disastrous.

The facts above reinforce the reasons why some countries ban the keeping or trade of Giant African Land Snails, although when kept responsibility as pets they should hopefully cause none of these problems.

Chapter 2: Housing the snails

1. Enclosure

Glass has the benefit of being more scratch resistant and scratches in plastic containers can make it difficult to clean. Plastic, in general, is lighter and more robust. My personal preference is for a glass tank but each to their own.

As a general rule, Giant African Land Snails need an enclosure that is at least three times the length of the snail itself in both width and depth. Adequate space is necessary for all Achatinidae. Studies have shown that snails are 'stressed' when kept in cramped conditions ,which (even when sufficient food is available) manifests itself as a reduction in growth rate. Second-hand aquariums (with the addition of ventilation holes in the lids where required) tend to make affordable and practical homes for Giant African Land Snails.

2. Temperature

Although originally from a tropical climate, Giant African Land Snails seem to adapt well to low heat. In the Bonin Islands south of Japan, winter temperatures are typically as low as 7°C, and A. fulica survives thereby entering a state of dormancy, like hibernation, 10–12.5cm (4-5in.) below the soil surface. In captivity, their tank can be kept anywhere from 65-84°F (18-29°C), but 70-79°F (21-26°C) is a good range to aim for.

Important features of the housing system:

- Must have enough space, well ventilated and well drained
- Have easy access to tend the snails, escape proof and keep out predators.
- Should be constructed with available, affordable, inexpensive and durable materials.

However, in Nigeria for example, snail farmers have developed many innovative systems of housing snails. A typical snail housing system consists of:

- a Rectangular dwarf wall made of concrete blocks (about two blocks from ground level).
- ½ inch wire netting for the body and roofing.
- Skeletal framework of iron bars (planted to avoid rusting) - Mosquito netting (nylon) - 30cm deep gutter around the house filled with water to prevent crawling ants from getting into snailery.
- Dwarf plants such as cocoyam, bitter leaf, waterleaf, etc.
- Located under a shaded tree or plant to climb and cover the body and top of the building.
- Dry leaves of banana, plantain, cocoa, etc.
- Provide containers (flat) for water and feed; the environment should look as natural as possible.

Other standard housing systems include:

- Cage or Hutch box –
- Fenced pen
- Pots or drums
- Used tires.

SUMMARY of accommodation FOR SNAILS: The type of house used depends on the volume of the business undertaken. However, avoid overstocking.

a) For 10 to 20 Snails; Use Old tires. 3 to 4 old tires laid on one another and covered with plastic or wire netting.

b) Earthen pot: Big and profound cover with plastic or wire mesh.

c) For 20 and above snails: Raised Wooden Cage.Stand it in a container filled with old engine oil to deter insect crawlers.

d) For 100 and above-Concrete trench: Concrete channel made of 2 coaches cement blocks high. The upper part of 2ft or more high to be constructed with planks and zinc or; chicken wire covered with plastic or wire netting of the trench should be concrete. Fix a good cover with a padlock.

Partition the trench into roosting area, feeding area and hatchery box located above the roosting area. Clean the Trench regularly as well as pick the eggs and bury in the sand in the hatchery which must not be allowed to dry out. If you must enter the pen, step on locks to avoid crushing snail eggs.

Chapter 3: Buying the snails

Before you buy your snails, or any other pet for that matter, ensure you can provide the correct environment for its needs. Also be aware that all pets require a degree of care and commitment. If you are not prepared to give this at the start and throughout the life of the animal, then do not buy the pet.

Obviously, where you are in the world has an impact on what is available locally - be that species or color types, etc., but there are some different buying options available to the potential snail keeper.

You can judge a pet shop on the general premises and enclosures the animals are kept in, and this is not just the Giant African Land Snail tanks themselves. Of course, holding areas will be smaller than at home due to space constraints and their temporary nature, but they should be safe, clean and in good overall condition. Avoid buying from pet shops or breeders who keep their stock in small enclosures - it does not bode well for the snails themselves.

There are also some things to look for when buying snails from a pet shop; these include:

- A real snail will be out of the shell moving around the enclosure and moving around for food.

- The foot of the snail should be moist to the touch.

- The round will be relatively clean and free from dirt.

- The snail's shell should not have signs of any cracks or breaks. Buying online and unseen is always a risk, but there are many good suppliers on the Internet. Vendors who have a physical presence, for instance, a high street pet shop that is too far for you to visit but also sells online, is a safer bet than a purely online business. That said there are good and bad in every industry and some of the best specimens can be procured from small private breeders. Many online exotic pet forums now exist and asking an experienced member of these forums for their advice, or using a search engine to find reviews of suppliers is a good way of finding out the standard of any stock you may receive.

It is worth bearing in mind that some unscrupulous sellers know the increased value of unusual species or color morphs and many snails are sold knowingly incorrectly labeled to increase the asking price. On one popular online auction site recently, I have seen young A. fulica being marketed as the rarer and therefore more expensive A. Zanzibar ice. Do your research, buyers beware!

Chapter 4: Feeding the snails

Many people will think you feed your snails lettuce and cucumber every day, and theoretically, you could do this but this food would hold little or no nutritional value. Providing vegetables rich in color and flavors will help your snail try new foods and develop a "cultured palette."

Place bread in a food bowl or plate. Your snail will sense and find the food themselves but you can also pick them up and put them near to the food and they will soon tuck into it and munch away. Snails eat slowly and in small amounts unless it is a favourite food of theirs so don't worry if they munch a little bit then slide off for a while, they will often come back for another munch or if they are feeling full up they may not eat a great deal in one day. Usually snails will eat all day every day, so it's a perfect way to introduce new and exciting foods. Try to add 2-3 different types of food per day, so I suppose you could call that "breakfast, lunch and dinner, " and usually we do have to wake our snails up for food because they love to burrow and sleep for hours!

1. A list of foods that your snail can eat:

It isn't a definitive list, but we have produced this list to provide a balanced and rich diet.

☐ Cucumber (One of their favorites)

☐ Lettuce (Holds little nutritional value though)

- ☐ Green beans (My snail LOVES them)
- ☐ Apples
- ☐ Bananas
- ☐ Red, green and orange peppers
- ☐ Blueberries
- ☐ Blackberries (Although these may be an acquired taste)
- ☐ Butternut squash
- ☐ Cabbage
- ☐ Carrot
- ☐ Cherry
- ☐ Dandelion leaves
- ☐ Soaked dog biscuits
- ☐ Soaked porridge oats
- ☐ Lettuce
- ☐ Kiwi
- ☐ Mango
- ☐ Melon
- ☐ Peas
- ☐ Peaches
- ☐ Plum
- ☐ Potato
- ☐ Sweetcorn
- ☐ Raisins (another acquired taste)
- ☐ Tomato
- ☐ Turnip
- ☐ Watermelon

These foods can be offered by themselves or mixed.

They may also feed during the day when it rains or when there are dark clouds. The quantity of feeds required is about 10% of the body weight, i.e., a snail of 100g requires 10g of feed per day. Feeding is usually done in the evening while moldy and left-over food should be removed daily.

Food having an offensive odor must be avoided. The combination of different feeds is highly recommended. Table salt is prohibited and give water leaf with caution, please.

Types of food are arranged as follows:

Leaves: Pawpaw, Cocoyam, Cassava, Okra, Cowpea, eggplant, waterleaf.

Tubers: Cocoyam, Cassava, white yam, sweet potato.

Fruit: Pawpaw, mango, banana, plantain, eggplant, pear, oil palm, tomato, sweet orange, guava, pineapple, coconut.

Grains: ground maize, guinea corn, and millet.

Industrial by-products: Wheat Offals, rice bran, Soya bean residue.

Household wastes: Peels of banana, plantains, pawpaw, pineapple, pounded yam, amala, eba, fufu, cooked rice, beans (all these must be without salt).

Snails require a lot of calcium, which should be provided in the form of powder, the ground of burnt, snail shell, poultry egg shell or bone meals industrial lime chalk (white).

- Blood meal and fish meal with providing protein. (Please ensure there is no salt).

- Clean water contained in the shallow container. Rain, well or river water is preferred, and must be provided at all times.

2. Foods to avoid

Citrus fruit such as lemons, oranges, and tangerines are far too sharp for snails and will cause them serious health problems. Their stomachs cannot cope with digesting these citrus flavors and it may put your snail off eating in the future.

Vegetables such as spinach and avocado are high in oxides and generally should be avoided.

NEVER feed them pasta in any form or style as this will bloat their stomachs and could even kill your snail. Bread should be avoided too, especially white bread but a small piece of brown bread soaked in water should be ok for a treat.

Finally, the thing everyone seems to know about snails is that they like beer! Yes, they do but they like the yeast in it rather than the beer, and again we recommend this only as a rare and small treat. A teaspoon of beer in their feeding bowl or a few drops on the end of a clean damp finger is delicious and your snail will love it.

Following these guidelines, your snail will be able to have a delicious, varied and safe diet.

Any food that is still in the bowl 24-36 hours after placing it in there should ideally be removed and thrown away, and foods such as bananas will ripen and go "off" quicker than other foods.

3. Fun with food

It's important that you experiment with food and introduce new flavors and foods to your snails diet, so they don't become complacent or fussy. As a bit of fun, we have created some straightforward and easy recipes for you to try.

Potato and vegetable mash

One small partially cooked/softened new potato

Half a green bean

Sprinkles of broccoli

Crush the potato into a thick paste in a dish. Mix the peas, green bean and broccoli and sprinkle into the mash. Present the mixture in small lumps or flatten it out in their food bowl. This recipe will give the snail their green vegetable intake as well as the nutrients from the potatoes.

Fruit Porridge

A few oats

Two types of fruit such as apples and strawberries.

Mix the oats with water to make a small amount of porridge (depending on how many snails you're making it for) and pour it into the food bowl. Chop chunks of apple and strawberry and drop them into the porridge mixture. This thick sweet mixture will be a firm favorite with your snails.

"Meat and two veg"

A small amount of raw mince meat

Cauliflower

Cabbage

Mix the raw meat with the two vegetables. You may need to add a little water to the meat mix to make it a bit more digestible for your snail. Snails do like meat every now and again, and this is another great way to introduce new vegetables too.

"Traffic light salad"

Red pepper

Yellow pepper

Green pepper

Grapes

Cut the peppers into half slices and the grapes into halves or quarters. Mix the peppers and grapes together to make a bright, colorful salad similar to "red, yellow and green" traffic lights. Easy and straightforward and pepper is extremely beneficial to shell colouration and development.

"Beer bananas"

To be given as treat only

Small amount of beer and bananas mixed together.

Achatinidae are regarded as herbivores, feeding primarily on living and decaying plants. They are typically unfussy eaters using their radula, a tooth-covered rasp to scrape and cut away food. In fact, according to Ademolu et al. (2004) in their studies with A. fulica, snails can be fed on poultry droppings and seem to fair pretty well - although I cannot recommend that diet myself!

Each snail typically eats approximately 10% of their weight daily. Working this out accurately is probably more trouble than it is worth and just providing a range of foodstuffs in sufficient amounts, so there is always something for them to eat likely to be a good pragmatic approach.

Giant African Land Snails benefit from calcium supplementation in their diet. Calcium is used for a plethora of biological processes, such as within the nervous system, growth, and maintenance of their shells and it is also employed in the shell of their eggs. Studies have also shown increased mortality in snails living on lower calcium diets. Taking this all into account, it's best practice to always provide a piece of a cuttlebone or another calcium source (such as empty chicken eggshells) with their food.

However, a very shallow bowl can be provided - one designed for reptile vivariums with stepped edges is ideal to keep the snail from slipping into the water. The liquid should be replaced regularly, and the bowl kept clean to prevent mold growth and disease.

Snails are primarily herbivores but will eat almost anything. They love fresh vegetables and fruits and plant life. Therefore, it's important for your snail habitat to contain lots of leafy vegetables, including sweet potatoes, paw plants, cabbage, tomatoes, cucumbers, and beans. If you can grow it in a home garden, snails will eat it, and if the plant has large leaves, it will provide shade as well as food for your snails.

For special snail treats, apples, pears, and other fruits and vegetables can also be tossed into the snail enclosure. However, before you feed your snails produce from your local supermarket, make sure it is organic or washed very thoroughly. Pesticides and chemicals used in food for human consumption can hurt your snails.

To promote healthy snails and provide them with essential vitamins and minerals for their shells, supplements can also be scattered around the enclosure, including blood and bone meal, crushed limestone, chalk, wood ash and ground oyster, and egg shells.

Saving Money on Snail Food

Growing your vegetables inside your snail habitat can save money on snail food. Also, if you grow them in a separate garden, excess vegetables can be fed to the snails, providing they were not sprayed with insecticides or pesticides.

Speeding Up Snail Growth

Snails grow faster and reproduce more often when they are fed well, and it is not uncommon for a snail to eat up to 3 percent of their body weight in any given 24 hour period. Plus, giant snails are worth more because they contain more meat.

Snails And Fat Content

Over feeding snails does not result in a snail with a high-fat content. Instead of becoming fat, snails naturally grow larger.

Notes About Feeding

Snails taste like what they eat. Therefore, the fresher the food and the more fresh fruits and vegetables you feed your snails, the better they will feel.

Snails should never receive food with salt in it. Salt dehydrates the snail and can kill it.

Chapter 5: Heating, temperature and substrates for the enclosure

Keep an eye on temperatures, especially in winter. If it is too cold then the snails will curl into their shell, and you won't see them which is no fun for a household pet. Try to avoid keeping them in colder rooms such as conservatory or sheds, however if this is the only place you can keep them then buying a heat mat is recommended. Heat mats must ALWAYS be bought with a thermostat to ensure temperatures are controlled and kept safe for both the snail and your household. Giant snails are from a naturally humid country and environment so spraying the substrate, the sides of the tank and even the snail itself with warm water is the perfect way of maintaining humidity, this should be done two to three times a day to provide optimum temperatures and using a spray bottle is ideal for this.

Use your snail as a guide in regards to temperatures and heating and if your snail is less active than usual or you notice a change in behavior or diet then looking into the temperature is an important avenue.

Substrates

Housing for a giant snail is simple, cheap and easy to set up. An ideal "house" for these animals is a plastic or glass tank. However, the plastic tank is proving very popular. These can be bought quickly into any reputable pet shop or reptile shop, an ideal plastic tank should be well ventilated with the lid having pre-made holes or slats, and it will usually include a small plastic opening for easy access. Once a tank is unpacked and set up, you will then need some form of substrate.

In regards to the substrate, the most popular choice is soil. The soil MUST be brought from a pet shop or reptile shop and will usually be found in the reptile section; this soil is clean, checked and most importantly safe. Other people may choose moss or even paper, but both substrates have their drawbacks, so we do recommend soil substrate.

The substrate should be spread along the bottom of the tank with at least 2-3 inches of it put in for the snails to burrow which is a natural trait and once evened out your tank is set up and ready to go! You can also include a sturdy reptile style bowl for feeding and bathing. Yes, it's as simple as that.

Chapter 6: Breeding and mating

As mentioned earlier, snails are "asexual" meaning they could, if needed, mate with themselves. However, captive land snails usually do require two land snails for the mating process to be entirely satisfied. The mating process is long and in depth, so we won't go into it here.

In regards to breeding, snails will naturally burrow and bury their eggs deep in the substrate therefore it is important that if you have two or more snails and are cleaning your tank out weekly you check the soil carefully for hidden eggs, they are usually small white/yellowish eggs buried and may appear individually but often in clutches. If you intend to keep the babies then remove the eggs to a separate container or tank and re-bury them carefully. In 2-3 weeks you will have baby snails, and we recommend you keep them in their tank until they are big enough to handle and move around safely. Baby snails can be fed the same food as adult snails but will obviously need smaller "mushier" portions.

If you do not intend on keeping the kids either due to the room, space or time constraints, then please follow this quick humane and most importantly, legal guide to disposing of them.

Place the bag in the fridge and 2-3 days later remove them and dispose of the bag. You can also boil and crush the eggs, but freezing is considered the most humane and quickest way. As mentioned earlier there are laws regarding baby snails, and it is illegal to release captive-born Giant African Land Snails into the wild.

Self-fertilisation does sometimes rarely occur but these 'virgin' snails provide clutches comprising fewer than about ten eggs, and most of these eggs are sterile. Any young snails that arise from these eggs rarely survive through to sexual maturity. So for all intents and purposes, cross-fertilisation is necessary for the laying of sufficient quantity and quality of eggs for successful breeding to take place.

Different species of Giant African Land Snails can breed at different ages. A. achatina is sexually mature at around 22 months. A. fulica becomes sexually mature at approximately one year from hatching, although in ideal growing conditions this can be as early as five months.

In most species of land snails, sexual maturity is thought to have been reached once a snail produces a ridge on the edge of its shell – known as a lip reflection. Interestingly, however, with Giant African Land Snails, shell growth continues for some time after their reproductive system has developed, although only sperm is produced during shell growth with both eggs and sperm being produced once shell growth had ceased and maturity has been reached.

Courtship (yes snails 'court'!) and breeding occurs almost exclusively at night and can last for up to seven and a half hours! Studies have shown that courtship progresses to the population in only 10% of cases, suggesting that snails are perhaps choosier than many people think! Successful breeding usually occurs between snails of a similar age and size.

After mating has taken place, eggs are usually deposited between 8 and 20 days later. Achatinidae have developed a reproductive strategy where they can store sperm to allow the fertilization of eggs at a later date, perhaps when environmental conditions are more favorable for their offspring's survival. A. fulica has been known to produce viable eggs over a year (382 days) after mating! Achatinidae deposit their eggs in 'nests' they excavate in the soil or their tank substrate, but occasionally they may only be stored on the ground in moist crevices among plant litter and stones.

The eggs of all species are spherical or elliptical in shape and are a chalky white to creamy yellow in colouration. A. zanzibarica and A. iradelei, as already stated, do not lay eggs as they give birth to live young. Sometimes, they give birth to a couple of dry or infertile eggs as well, but these will, of course, will not develop.

Giant African Land Snails are very prolific breeders. The number of eggs per clutch increases in correlation with age and size of the snail. Given the right conditions, a mature A. fulica can lay 900-1200 eggs each year! On the Philippine island of Bugsuk, an estimated 45 million A. fulica were collected and destroyed on just 4000 acres (16 square kilometers) of land over a seven month period! It's easy to see how Giant African Land Snails got their reputation as an invasive species!

In general, Achatina species lay the most amount of eggs, with up to 400 at a time (though not all of them are likely to hatch successfully). Due to both the snails being hermaphrodites, if mature, each snail is liable to lay fertilized eggs. These eggs are creamy white and relatively small, about 5mm (0.1in) in length. Moisture and temperature effect the overall incubation period in all species. Incubation times are further complicated by inconsistent degrees of ovoviviparity in egg clutches, or in plain English, eggs with young snails in different stages of development can be laid; hence the period of hatching varies. Damp substrate in relatively warm conditions ensures the best hatch rates.

When the young snails are a hatch, they appear as miniature adults. There is no metamorphosis from a different form or molting as with some invertebrate species. After emerging from the egg, snails remain underground with other members of the clutch for several days. During this time the hatchlings consume their eggshells and sometimes the eggshells of unhatched siblings gaining valuable calcium. Young snails grow from the mantle of the shell adding material to the leading edge of the tank, which in turn adds more whorls.

Fungal growth on the eggs can cause hatching problems, especially in the damp warm conditions the snails enjoy. Removal of the egg clutch to sterile and moistened cotton wool or sawdust can reduce this issue. On the whole though in a domestic setting, fungus does not pose a significant problem to hatch rates.

Of course, few snail keepers will want to raise all these eggs to adulthood, so the question as to what to do with them soon becomes apparent. A snail keeper has some avenues open to him or her:

- Keep every last snail hatchling! Turning your whole house into a massive snail-atrium, which slowly takes over your entire life- or maybe not
- Breed them for your local pet shop or garden center to sell. If you do this, to avoid disappointment, make sure the store in question agrees to it beforehand. Do not expect to get rich from selling snails!
- Sell them to your friends (unless you have a lot of friends this isn't probably a long term solution).
- Freeze the eggs (as discussed above). When disposing of the eggs after this process makes sure that there is no possible chance that they could still hatch as it is illegal for them to be released into the environment, even if it was not intentional!

If you are keeping the baby snails, it is best to separate the adults from the eggs and the babies as they could accidentally damage them.

Chapter 7: Health

1. Routine practices for healthy snails

a) Adequate feeding at regular intervals daily with their preferred feeds and with other high-quality food materials.

b) Proper watering of the snail and the housing units at least once daily, and more frequently during the dry season to prevent snails from aestivating during which they stop feeding and growth. The watering utensils should be washed regularly.

c) Regular cleaning of the housing units by removing remnants and decaying feeds, which may attract insects into the snailery.

d) Daily inspection of snails to ensure that they are active and well, that there is no harmful organism hiding anywhere in the house, that newly laid eggs or newly hatched babies are collected promptly and taken care of.

e) Regular Cleaning of the surrounding of the snailery to remove weeds, which may harbor snails pest and predators.

f) Exercising caution on the use of salty feed and water, as snails cannot naturally tolerate much salt.

g) Prompt removal of dead or inactive snails to prevent cross infection in case of possible disease infection.

h) Proper illumination of the snailery and the surroundings for easy detection of snail enemies wandering around and to allow increased activity and feeding during the night.

i) Careful selection of high quality foundation stock by purchasing from a good source or by obtaining one's stock directly from a natural source.

j) Avoiding the use of fertilizers, compost and animal manure in the snail pen as such materials can burn the snail flesh.

2. Healthcare and handling

The snails are low maintenance, and captive snails will rarely experience health problems unless they are neglected or housed in the wrong conditions. A varied diet is essential for a snail to stay healthy, active and safe. Captive snails will require a constant source of calcium and the cheapest and easiest option is purchasing a pack of "cuttlefish bones" from pet shops to place in the tank for the snails to eat and build their intake up in order for their shells to stay vigorous and healthy, on average cuttlebones usually last 7-10 days and we recommend changing it over when you do the weekly clean. A weekly clean is recommend to keep conditions safe and clean and involves changing the substrate and wiping the tank clean with warm water, but please DO NOT use any soap or tank cleaner as these chemicals will harm your snail.

When handling your snail, ensure your hands are damp and fresh and free of soap or chemicals. Lift the snail by their shell and place them on their side. If the snail is climbing on the tank then lightly spray them so they slide off but please do not pull them off as you may damage them or even pull their shells off.

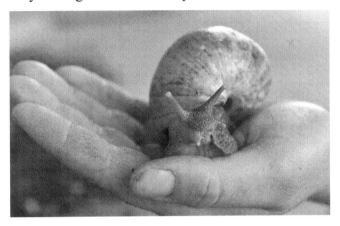

As snail owners, it's nice to spend some "out of tank" time with your snail. You can hold them in your hand, but we use trays to allow them to crawl around exploring new surroundings and again ensure the plate is wet or damp for the snail to feel comfortable and to keep them moist. Snails also love baths and showers but be careful with how much water you're using, you can hold the snail in your hand and lightly run the shower head over your snail which they will love and lap up the water. This is also an ideal time to get an old toothbrush or tissue and clean the shell gently to remove mud and substrate.

Although no one has had a response from asking them directly, snails do not seem to mind being handled. The shell is most fragile at the base where it is next to the body, so try to avoid picking them up by this part, and be careful to provide substantial support to the body and shell.

In simple terms, Giant African Land Snails do not have teeth that can bite. Instead, they have a rough tongue called a radula, which has distinct ridges on it so that snails grasp their food rather than chewing or eating it. When handling, you can sometimes feel a snail grating your skin. It is a slightly rough, tickly sensation but it cannot do you any harm. Snails seem to grasp most surfaces they come across, checking to see if things are edible.

3. Cleanliness

Giant African Land Snails should be treated with the same care and attention to cleanliness as any other pet, like birds, snakes, terrapins, tortoises, etc.

Giant African Land Snails are hardy animals and keeping them in clean and appropriate conditions probably helps alleviate the majority of the possible health issues.

4. Hibernation and Aestivation

Hibernation and estivation are not health matters in the truest sense. Hibernation is a state of inactivity or reduction of bodily processes in warm-blooded (endothermic) animals due to reduced temperatures. As Giant African Land Snails are cold-blooded (ectothermic), they cannot hibernate in the truest sense of the word (although they can aestivate) but they have coping strategies for when their environments become too cold, too hot or too dry.

Giant African Land Snails will go into a state of dormancy if temperatures get too low, and aestivate when temperatures are too high or too dry (Barker 2002). In principle, these two mechanisms look very similar. Feeding stops, the snails will retract into their shells and a crusty membrane forms to protect the snail from losing water. This temporary layer is known as an epiphragm and is made from dried mucus. Studies in India, by Rahman and Raut (2012), have shown that during this period of dormancy the heart rate of the snails was reduced by 85% and the oxygen consumption went down by 83% allowing the snails to survive extended periods of severe environmental conditions. They cannot, however, survive forever in this state, and many snails kept in unsuitable conditions sadly fail to 'wake up' from this dormancy.

In general, a period of hibernation or aestivation can be overcome by altering the environment of the snails. E.g. providing additional heat or cooling through ventilation as needed to bring temperatures back to the 'safe' range for the species. Spray the enclosure with water to increase humidity levels back to 'normal' levels. Although it is important to bear in mind too much water is as bad for the snails as not enough!

Many people try to 'wake' their dormant snails with warm baths or showers, but I feel this may shock the snails with the sudden change in conditions. Unhurried incremental variations in the snail's immediate environment and letting nature take its course more slowly is probably the healthiest method for your snail.

5. Mites

Occasionally, small fast moving white or creamy mites can be seen crawling on the snails and within the tank itself. These are commonly Riccardoella limp cum or another similar Acari (or mite) species, which were once thought to be fairly benign; feeding on shed skin cells and mucus. New research now suggests they may also feed on the snail's blood. They probably don't present a significant health concern to an otherwise healthy snail (or a person for that matter!), and wild populations of snails possess these tiny 'passengers, ' but they might cause problems in high numbers or contribute to the weakening of an already ill snail. Not to mention some people find them unsightly. The best way to remove them is to keep the snail's enclosure very clean, replacing substrate regularly and giving the affected snails baths in lukewarm water to gently wash the mites away.

6. Poisoning

The skin of all snail species is very porous, and they will absorb nearly anything on the surface of their enclosure. You must, therefore, keep chemicals, such as deodorants, paint, cleaning agents and flea sprays away from your snail and its enclosure, as these can cause poisoning and ultimately death for your pet. When feeding your snails, you should also ensure that all items are washed thoroughly to stop pesticides, fertilizers and other chemicals harming your pets

7. Shell Breakage

Snails do restore broken parts of their shell and heal over small breaks in their shells if kept in good clean conditions and provided with a good varied diet, high in calcium, to provide the snails the means to heal itself. That said, like any living creature, some accidents cannot heal on their own and professional help may be required.

The increase in exotic pet keeping has meant veterinarians are becoming more experienced with dealing with unusual species such as Giant African Snails and if you feel a snail is severely damaged or unwell, a trip to the vets may be beneficial.

Chapter 8: Snail licenses and farm permits

Have you ever considered snail farming? Certain types of snails are considered delicacies and can be raised on farms or small parcels of land and sold for a profit. Snails are incredibly easy to breed. Each snail is capable of laying between 45 and 60 eggs at a time, and some snails lay eggs more than one time a year. It can result in thousands of snails each year and large profits once they are sold.

Starting a snail farm is incredibly comfortable. All you need is fertile, moist dirt, several vegetable plants, herbs, and bushes and a fencing system to keep out pests and bugs, buyers for your snails, and a willingness to do a little research on caring for and breeding snails.

1. Business Licenses

For a snail farm that intends to sell snails to the general populace, across state lines, and to restaurants and grocery stores, a business license may be needed. It's important to check local state and city regulations to determine if your snail farm needs a business license.

2. Snail Farm Permits

In some areas, a permit to raise, import, and sell snails may be needed. It is because some snails can be considered invasive and a pest, and the local authorities want to ensure that you are raising your snails correctly and not letting them escape into the local environment, where they could cause harm to the ecosystem.

3. Benefits of Raising Your Snails

Raising snails can be a rewarding, profitable, and delicious experience. Snail meat is prized across the globe, and it is much cheaper to come to your snails than it is to purchase snails in a grocery store or as a dinner entrée at a restaurant.

Raising snails is also environmentally friendly when done correctly. Snails do not require the use of pesticides and insecticides, and they are not typically an environmental hazard. Some further benefits include:

· Free/Low-Cost Food
· Economically Viable
· Environmentally Friendly
· Potential To Make Money

Chapter 9: Housing Your Pet Snail

There are many different options for housing your pet snail. Below I will discuss the most popular options, and the equipment you will need.

1. Trench Pen

A trenched pen is constructed by digging a rectangular trench measuring 3 meters in length, 2-meter breath and 70 meters thick on the ground. The pen may be single or with many compartments based on your needs and imagination. The side of the pen should be built with sand concrete blocks; the lid should be made of wire netting.

Disadvantages:

- Uncomfortable working posture.
- Danger of predators of gaining access with ease on the animals
- Flooding of the housing unit is not unlikely

2. Fenced Cage

It is built based on your taste, but hardwood of mahogany must be used and durable wire net mesh. The base should be wood, and the top must be made with lids made of timber and wire mesh.

This is the recommended housing for your GALS.

3. Old Motor Tires

Used tyres are also used to rear snails, two or three tyres should be placed on the bare floor (loamy soil). Then cover it with a wood made wire net mesh for easy opening and accessing, and you could fill each tyre hole with loamy soil for easy breeding.

Note: Maximum of two or three tires should be used.

If you are going to try this on a concrete floor, the need to fill it with loamy soils is important before you add the tire, changing the soli every two weeks will arise.

4. Basket

Baskets can also be used to rear snails, either indoors or outdoors, but the issue is baskets don't last long, so I don't and won't advise the use of basket.

The basket has to be filled with loamy or humus soil before the snails are introduced into the basket, but the lid of the bucket must be covered with wire meshing made with wood or a plastic cover to prevent the snail from escaping and a weighty item be placed on it to hold it firm.

5. Drums and Pots

The bottom of the drums or containers must be perforated for breathing of the animals, humus or loamy soil must be introduced into the pan and covered with banana leaves, before the introduction of the snails. As usual, the drums or pots (clay pots) must be covered with wire net mesh.

6. Choosing the Site

The site to build your snail farm should be very fertile, drain well, and contain lots of light while still providing ample shade.
The primary litmus test for a good snail site is whether or not the soil is capable of supporting a vegetable garden.

7. Finding the Site

There should be enough room to build between one and three 15' by 15' snail pens. A beginning snail farmer may only want to create one snail pen to start their operation. It is so that they can raise a few hundred snails the first year and learn about snail farming through hands-on experience.

Building more than one pen to start may prove to be overwhelming to a beginning snail farmer, especially if he or she plans to be the sole employee at the business.

8. Preparing the Soil for your pen

Mark the area you intend to use with stakes and twine. Make the land as you would a garden. Remove all the grass trees and roots from the area. Do not only dig the grass out of the soil and turn it over. You must completely remove all plant life and grass, including the roots. When you finish, you should only see and feel the dirt.

Throw the roots, rocks, and any trees away, but save the plants and grass. The plant material will be needed later to sterilize and fertilize the soil.

If it does not flow, the soil needs to be raised above the water line, and sand needs to be tilled into the ground. To increase the dirt level above the water line, add several inches of topsoil. Once the new soil has been added, test the area again with more water. Repeat until the soil drains well.

Next, it's time to add the grass and saved organic material to the ground. Make sure it completely and evenly covers the area. Do not leave any open dirt. If the plants and grass do not cover the area, use leaves or other plants from other regions.

Once the material is laid, clear two to three feet around the outside of the pen and create a path with either gravel or paver stones or make sure the area is not flammable and provide a convenient walkway to monitor and tend to your snails.

Next, wait for the grass, leaves, and plant material to completely dry. Once it is dry, set it on fire and monitor the fire. The burning of the dried organic material will cleanse the ground of all harmful insects and any remaining weeds and invasive seeds. It will rid the area of mice, rats, shrews, and other small rodents and pests, and it will create a rich, organic topsoil.

Once the fire is out and cooled, toss the soil again, ensuring that it is loose to a depth of six to eight inches. You are now ready to build your snail pen.

9. Building the Snail Pen

Snails need to be in a clean, pest-free environment. Therefore, as soon as the fire is out and the soil tilled, immediately begin building the fencing that will surround your snail farm. If too much time elapses from the fire and tilling to building, bugs, pests, and rodents can re-enter the area, resulting in the need to burn and farm again.

10. Tools and Building Materials

· Posts

· Chicken Wire, woven fencing, corrugated plastic, or corrugated metal

· Hammer

· Nails or screws

· Sledgehammer or mallet

The goal is to build a fence that will not allow bugs, rodents, or other pests into your snail farming area and to prevent snails from leaving the area and entering the yard and local ecosystem. Chicken wire and posts alone will create an adequate fence. Although it may keep out large rodents and other small mammals and lizards, it is not stable enough to prevent insects and mice from entering the area, and your snails could escape through the holes in the chicken wire and cause damage to nearby plants, gardens, and agricultural areas.

The wall should come up out of the ground by at least two feet.

11. Chicken Wire and Woven Fencing

Using chicken wire and a woven fencing material like basket weaved wood or vinyl can provide enough protection for your snails, and it's the cheapest way to build a snail enclosure. The trick to this method is to purchase chicken wire with the smallest holes possible and put that around the snail growing area first. Next, put up the woven fencing, ensuring it is tight enough to keep out bugs and other pests. Dirt will need to be filled in on both sides to provide a tight seal from the fence to the ground.

It should be noted that if organic woven fencing materials are used, they will eventually rot and decay and require replacing. Some snail farmers, who use natural fencing materials, split their fencing in half lengthwise. They screw or nail the top of the fence in place then add the lower level of fencing. This is so that they do not have to remove and replace the entire fence when the bottom half rots. It makes the repairs easier to perform and reduces maintenance costs.

12. Corrugated Plastic or Metal

Purchasing corrugated plastic or metal is more expensive than chicken wire and woven fencing materials, but it is a much more secure fencing option. To install this option, place the posts around the snail growing area, leaving 12 to 16 inches between posts.

Staple, nail, or screw the corrugated material to the fence posts with some overlap between the sheets. Spacing the sheets at any distance or leaving cracks between layers can give bugs, pests, and rodents an opportunity to enter your snail farm.

13. Greenhouses

Snails can also be grown in greenhouses, which can be purchased at any local home improvement store. Greenhouses typically come with everything needed to build the greenhouse, and the humidity, soil temperatures, and moisture are much easier to control in a greenhouse.

To establish habitats in a greenhouse, only make small snail pens along the dirt floor and prepare the soil as if you were raising snails outside, or put dirt and plants into raised beds within the greenhouse.

After the beds, soil, and plants are installed in the greenhouse, raising the snails is the same as raising them outside in outdoor pens, except there is less chance of pests, insects, and invasive plants and weeds infiltrating the greenhouse.

Chapter 10: Types of snails

There are five main types of snail that are perfect for farming and selling as food, including the Garden Snail, Roman Snail, Cabrales, Wood Snail, and Escargo Turn. These snail breeds are safe to eat and considered delicacies in most parts of the world.

1. Petit Gris/Common Garden Snail

Petit Gris snails are also known as small brown snails or Garden Snails. The Garden Snail's official name is Helix Aspersa, and it originated in the Mediterranean and Western Europe. Through transportation, both intentional and unintentional, this snail can now be found all over the world. Unfortunately, though edible, it is often considered a pest in gardens and agricultural businesses, and proper permits must be acquired before raising this breed.

Garden Snails grow between 25 and 35 mm tall and are typically brown or brownish-grey in color. They eat plant and plant materials.

These snails are sometimes hunted by birds and other animals and rodents and eaten. Therefore, it is imperative to protect them from predators.

Reproduction can occur both sexually and asexually. However, these snails prefer mating via their "love horns." Mating occurs simultaneously between both snails. Each snail lays between 60 and 80 eggs and can reproduce up to six times a year. Snails take between 12 and 24 months to fully mature. They can live up to 25 years. These snails can acquire parasites if not properly cared for and fed.

2. Roman Snail

The Roman Snail's official name **is** Helix Pomatia, and it's one of the most common snails grown for escargot. It grows between 30 and 45 mm in height and prefers garden and vineyard habitats. The egg laying season begins at the end of May and extends until the end of July. They do not require mates to breed, but they have been known to produce with partners. Between 40 and 65 eggs can be expected per snail.

Roman Snails primarily eat leaves and grass, and their feeding can be noted by small holes in the leaves.

They require at least two inches of loose soil to deposit their eggs and for hibernation in the winter. They reach full maturity in two to five years and can live up to 35 years.

3. Cabrales

The Cabrales snail's official name is Iberus Aloneness. These snails are so famous as escargot; they are considered endangered. They primarily reside in Spain, where they are harvested from the wild and sold to restaurants, grocery stores, and snail connoisseurs.

4. Wood Snail

The **Wood Snail** originated in Central Europe and have since spread across the globe. It thrives in nearly all environments and is one of the few snails that scavenge and eat dead snails, plants, and worms. Its official name is Cepaea Nemoralis, and it can survive in cold climates. This snail prefers dry, shady areas and will not thrive in overly wet, sunny locations. They prefer to live under rocks and along and inside the stems of plants and shrubs.

5. Escargo Turc

The Escargo Turc is also known as the Striped Roman Snail. This snail rose in popularity after the Roman Snail was listed as a protected species, as a result of overharvesting. It is primarily located along the Black Sea and from Turkey to Yugoslavia, which is how it received its common name. They can survive and thrive anywhere except in very high altitudes. They prefer to reside in bushes and hedges and around and under plant-life.

Chapter 11: Purchasing and acquiring snails

The hardest part of starting a snail farm is finding the snails. There are very few local stores that sell live snails for farming. Most snails that are sold in pet shops and retail stores are aquatic snails.

1. Purchasing from a Local Snail Farmer

Another way to buy live snails is by finding a **snail farmer** who is willing to sell live snails to another farmer and potential competitor. When using this route, it's important to ask the farmer a few simple questions before choosing snails and making the purchase.

1. Where did you get your first snails?

2. What breeds do you have?

3. Do you have a business license and a permit to sell snails?

4. How long have you been raising snails?

The answers to these questions will tell you if you've found a legitimate snail farmer and will increase the likelihood of purchasing healthy, edible snails.

2. Pet Shops and Retail Locations

Most towns and cities do not contain stores that sell healthy, live snails for farming. If you wish to purchase your snails from a retail store, it may be best to look online and mail order your snails.

However, that comes with several risks, including receiving the wrong snails and snails dying in the mail.

3. Choosing Healthy Snails

Signs and symptoms of illnesses can be hard to find on snails, there are visible signs of injury that you can see. If a snail has a broken or cracked shell, open cuts or gashes along its foot, flat spots or overly puffy areas, it's best to leave that snail alone. Lethargic snails should also not be purchased.

4. Purchasing the Correct Number of Snails

For each 15 by 15-foot enclosure, 150 small snails and 25 medium to large snails can be purchased. Trying to grow more snails in pen could result in some of the snails dying or becoming sick, which naturally results in lost initial income and profit.

Chapter 12: Aspects of snail farming

If you do not want to raise Giant African Land Snails just as pets, you can always make businesses out of breeding and raising them. This will be discussed in the following chapter.

1. Maintenance

Snails need very little maintenance. However, snail farmers should be vigilant in checking for injured or sick snails. If injured or sick snails are noticed, they should be removed from the habitat and disposed of. Keeping injured and infected snails inside your habitat could endanger the rest of your snails.

Snail Farmers should also keep an eye out for weeds, invasive grasses, and pests. If weeds or grass is noticed inside the habitat, it should be removed immediately. If pests are seen, the fence should be checked for rotting, wear and tear, and cracks. Defective areas of the wall should be replaced immediately, and the infestation should be dealt with in a way that does not harm the snails.

2. Initial Startup Cost

Snail farming is surprisingly affordable. The beginning snail farmer can expect to spend between $1,000 and $2,000 to prepare the ground, plant herbs, flowers, and vegetables for shade and snail food, and purchase the snails.

a] Building the Fence

Corrugated metal costs around $2.50 per linear foot. For a typical 15' by 15' snail pen, the total cost for the corrugated metal should be around $150 - $250. Two-foot fencing stakes can be purchased at any home improvement store for around $9 per bundle of 24. With stakes spaced at 12", the total cost for the stakes should be $18, which will provide enough stakes for one 15' by 15' pen with a few left over. It makes the maximum total cost for one snail pen $274, not including your choice of nails or screws. It also assumes that you are not paying yourself or anyone else to build the snail pen for you.

b] Excavating, Clearing, and Preparing the Land

Excavators and tillers can be rented from numerous heavy equipment rental facilities and home improvement stores. Self-propelled tillers cost $65 for four hours. A small excavator or bulldozer can be rented for about $440 for four hours. Assuming the land clearing and initial tilling can be performed within four hours, the total cost for land preparation is $945. Additional tilling and aerating will need to be conducted after the soil is cleansed with fire.

c] Two Foot Walkway around Snail Habitat

The cheapest and easiest way to create a walkway around your snail habitat is with gravel. A pickup truck load of gravel costs between $25 and $50 per ton. To create the walkway, remove all the grass, twigs, debris and rocks. Then, lay and spread the gravel. When finished, the walkway should be two inches thick and two feet wide. It makes monitoring and tending the snails much easier. It also prevents creeping grass and weeds from entering the snail habitat.

d] Truckload of Topsoil

If topsoil or fertile soil isn't available on the land, a truckload of topsoil can be purchased for about $250.

e] Snail Food and Plant Life

The cost of the plants residing inside the snail pen range in price according to whether seeds or plants are purchased. Seeds can be purchased for between $1 and $2.50 per pack, which is considerably cheaper than buying plants but can take longer because the plants have to grow and begin producing leaves and vegetables before the snails can be introduced.

Plants can be purchased for between $2.50 and $7 per biodegradable pot, which means that if you were to buy 35 plants, your total maximum cost would be $245. The benefit to purchasing plants instead of seeds is saved time. Transplanted flowers and vegetables are ready for snails in one to two weeks or as soon as they are established in their new soil.

If you opt to find your wild snails, there's no monetary cost. If they are purchased from a snail farmer, the price is up to the farmer. In general, you can expect to pay between $1 and $2 per snail. If 150 snails are purchased, the maximum cost would be $300.

3. Ongoing cost

a] Costs to Run the Farm

After the initial start-up costs, the costs to raise the snails are negligible and include replacing plants as they die and repairing and replacing fencing.

For farms that plan to offer processing and snail cleaning, costs could be incurred to buy cleaning equipment and packaging or paying a processing plant to process the snails for you.

b] Retail Snail Prices

Snails raised organically can be expected to fetch between $1 and $2 per snail or roughly the same prices that were paid to acquire the initial batch of snails.

c] Profits

Each snail lays between 45 and 60 eggs, the snail farmer can expect 6,750 new snails after the first year. Once hatched and out of the dirt, the first 150 snails can be sold for about $300. Assuming costs remain the same, each additional year will result in profits of up to $11,500, which makes snail farming incredibly lucrative, and if more snail pens are built, profits increase almost exponentially.

d] Business Planning and Financials

If you plan to run your snail farm as a profitable business, it's important to create a **business plan** and determine the demands of the local market. If individuals and local restaurants do not eat or serve snails, you won't have a very profitable business.

Also, you'll want to know what the start-up and maintenance costs are for your new business, the realistic profits and profit margins and create short and long-term goals. After all, a business that is not well-planned is twice as likely to fail within the first five years.

e] Entrepreneur Readiness

Snail farming, like all businesses, is demanding. It takes an individual who is dedicated to doing their business a success and willing to take control of their financial life. Small business owners need to be hands on. They need to wear many hats other than the business owner, including the manager, golfer, the buyer, accountant/Bookkeeper, marketing head, and account manager.

In the business of snail farming, the owner also has to be willing to feed, harvest, and care for the snails as well as ensure that their habitat remains clean and habitable.

Business plans can be presented to banks to facilitate the loan process. However, that's not why beginning snail farmers need a business plan. Small snail farms can be started with very little money, making the need for a loan obsolete. Instead, start-up snail farmers should create a business plan to give their snail farming operation a direction and definable goals with attainable benchmarks.

4. Do your business research

a] Create and Conduct a Market Survey

Before starting your farm, building a pen and purchasing snails, you will need to do a survey to ascertain the potential market for your snails and create a list of potential buyers. The questions should be worded very carefully so that you get the information you need to make an informed decision about the **snail market** in your area. Hand the survey out to at least 150 individuals and businesses that best represent the market you want to enter or the persons and businesses you wish to purchase your snails. Surveying a smaller sampling won't give you accurate results.

If the survey does not yield desirable results, a snail farming business may not be viable in your area. However, it's still possible to grow snails for your immediate and extended family's consumption.

b] Mission Statement

It should be a one or two line sentence that describes the goals of your business.

For Example:

AYZ snail farm strives to provide the freshest and healthiest snails to grocery stores and restaurants at competitive prices.

c] The Eterprise (Business Summary)

The next section should summarize your business and the plans you have for your business. This section should include a paragraph about your business objectives. It should list the founders of the business or key operating personnel. It should explain the history of the firm, and detail the business operations and provide future goals. Many business plan writers prefer to do this section last after they have worked out all the details of their activities and the financials.

d] The Market

This section is where your marketing survey is utilized to its full potential. In this section, you will need to discuss your market and projected market segment and growth potential. You will also need to state your environmental impact.

It's important to research and provide only facts in this section. Projected market segment should be foreshadowed using solid math and denoting areas that current snail farmers are neglecting.

Fudging or inventing numbers and market research does not help your business thrive, and it may give you a false sense of viability.

e] Business Offerings

The public offerings for a snail farm are live snails. However, snail farms can also offer to provide cleaned and processed snails that are pre-packaged. This section will also need to discuss the status of the current market, how your snail farm fits into that market, the value of the business, and the cost to produce and process the snails. It also helps if you can provide additional services that other snail farmers do not provide.

f] Marketing Strategy

What is your marketing strategy? Will you advertise and sell your snails online as well as from your farm? Will you create local advertising campaigns? How much will you charge for your snails? Will you offer bulk pricing?

This section is where you will determine how you will run your snail farm, the advertising costs, costs to produce the snails, and the retail prices of your snails. This section is significant for determining your profit margins and direct and indirect costs.

It will also explain how you plan to deliver your product to your customers and the types of customer service and support you plan to provide.

g] Initial Capital

This section should be dedicated to how you plan to fund the first few days and months of your snail farming operation. The money can be raised via on-line crowd-funding, family, and friends or taken from your savings and checking accounts.

Most snail farmers opt to pay for the initial costs of their farms out of their own pockets. It reduces their financial liability by eliminating costly loans and having to pay back friends and family, who many not be willing to wait for your farm to become profitable.

Another way to raise initial funds is by selling shares or percentages of your business. In this scenario, investors would be given signed contracts that state the percentage of the business they own.

h] Financial Projections

How much money do you expect your snail farming operation to bring in in the first year? How much income can you expect the second year? This section should be a dedicated year by year breakdown of expenses and revenues for the first five years. These estimates can be revised and rewritten to reflect the changing market demographics or a sudden, long-term demand for snail meat.

5. Keeping the business going

a] Business Plans Are Living Documents

Completing a business plan does not mean it is finished. Business plans should be reviewed, revised, and expanded at least once a year. Some companies even create objectives and goals 10 and 15 years ahead of time. It is to ensure that their businesses always have aims and objectives.

b] Frequency of Sales

Snail farms typically sell snails once a year after the baby snails have hatched and emerged from their holes. This provides lots of income at once, and snail farmers have to be very financially savvy to make that income last until the next snail harvest.

If enough snails do not sell, it may be necessary to cull the herd or build more snail habitats to prevent overpopulation of your pens.

c] Expansion

As your snail farm receives more frequent and larger orders, it may be necessary to expand operations to grow more snails. For farmers who started with one snail habitat, they may wish to build one or two more habitats after the first or second year.

It's also important to understand that each snail can produce hundreds produce of eggs each year. It, by itself, may fuel the need to build additional habitats.

6. Selection of foundation stocks

a) Begin with fully grown, sexually mature medium size snail.

b) Choose the same species and keep different species separately.

c) Choose only snails that fill their shells.

d) Avoid wounded snail or broken shell or drilled for passing a rope.

e) Avoid over-sized snails. They may be too old and will not lay much egg.

f) Farm snails common in your area to ensure acceptability and good market price and patronage.

7. Limiting factors

1. Overstocking: Not more than five snails per square meter are recommended. However, recent studies had shown that up to 10 snails per square meter are possible. However, completion and pollution of the environment may result from over stocking.

2. Environmental Pollution by mucus and faeces: Soils should be changed every three months in the case of the cage system while two years will be ideal for washing and cleaning up the free system.

3. Predators: Rats, frog, birds, snakes, lizards, centipedes, beetles, ants termites, cockroaches, and poachers are the primary predators of snails.

4. Parasites: flies should be prevented from gaining entry into the snailery.

5. Aestivation: The snail withdraws into its shell and seals up with a white calcareous layer to prevent loss of water from the body. This can be avoided by constant watering during the dry season.

6. Salt: Snails should not be fed with a diet containing salt and should never be allowed to come in contact with it, lest they die. Also avoid the use of fertilizers and pesticides in the snailery, as these may be harmful to the snails.

8. Advantages of snail rearing

a) High potential for huge returns with small inputs.
b) Easy handling of operation even by women and children.
c) Easy to combine with the normal schedule of service of a government worker.
d) Easy to operate without fear of injury from snails.
e) Brings additional income to the family.
f) Improve the health of the household.
g) Prevents the depletion and gradual extinction of the native snail population.

9. Marketing

Snail farmers can produce both for the local and export market. Many countries in Europe and America import both live and prepared snails. In 1978, imported live snails worldwide were estimated at $36 million. There is no doubt that the trade has increased ever since. It is important however to identify the would-be overseas customers and their reliability. An agreement must be reached between producer and consumers, and this agreement must be religiously adhered to. You must check the rules and regulations of the countries you are selling your snails to.

10. Harvesting snails

There are two ways to harvest snails. The first way involves waiting until the young snails have emerged from their holes and then collecting the older snails from your snail garden. There is no need to keep older snails on your farm, and not selling them could lead to an overpopulation of your habitat.

The second way to harvest snails is by removing them from their hibernation holes mid-fall or about one to two weeks after they have gone into hibernation for the winter. The French prefer this method because the snails are not active, easy to find, and fat. They also haven't been eating. If the snails are harvested before they go into hibernation, the snail farmer must remove the snail from their habitats and purge them before selling or cooking them.

Chapter 13: The Health Dangers of snails

Well we can all say that snails look pretty harmless to the human eye. You might just think that they're harmless yourself. I mean where is the harm? They are real slow, so they can't chase you in anyway, they don't have claws, so they can't scratch you, they can't bite you because their teeth are only designed to cut vegetation, so they can't leave bite marks on your skin because your hand is not a piece of lettuce.

They look so fascinating whenever you just watch them slither along with their antennas sticking out, and moving up and down, and sometimes left to right. With all that being said people think that they are really harmless, but actually the slow critter that has no way to physically attack anyone has a deep dark secret. No they can't bite or scratch anyone, but they carry diseases. Most people would probably guess salmonella being that it's the most popular disease among animals especially with cold blooded animals, and yes snails and slugs do carry salmonella, but they also carry a disease that is much, much worse than salmonella.

The disease that I'm referring to is called the rat round lung worm. The reason why the rat round lung worm is so scary is because the rat round lung worm is not really a disease, but a parasite. Snails and slugs are hosts for the rat round lung worm parasite, and that parasite causes meningitis (which is swelling of the membranes surrounding the brain). By now I would have to say that many people in Florida know about the rat round lung worm living inside of snails and slugs from the news on the Internet, and from watching television informational shows such as Monsters inside me.

A few years ago, the Giant African Land Snail was on the news, and the reporters were basically saying that not only are they eating up people's gardens, but they can make people sick with meningitis. It freaked the public out so much that lab workers went to people's houses looking for the Giant African Land Snail so that they could remove them out of their yards. The thing is the Giant African Land Snail looks like just any average yard snail, so it's hard to tell the difference between which snail is which, so people didn't know it was the Giant African Land until the snail grew larger and larger. Well the Giant African Land Snail story got everyone worked up to where there were other reality stories about people getting the rat round lung worm from any land snail or slug.

Well my guess is that people are now freaked out because they are afraid of getting the rat round lung worm from snails and slugs, so they might go to extreme measures to keep snails and slugs out of their yards and keeping little kids indoors in fear of their kids getting sick.

However, in my perspective people forget how snails and slugs get the parasite in the first place. If you listen to the word "rat round lung worm" you can easily guess where the snails and slugs get the parasite from- from rats. The process is quite simple. A rat infected with the rat round lung worm eventually does his business by laying droppings. The snail or slug eats the droppings and the snail or slug is now a host of the parasite, and capable of infecting humans with the parasite.

Now that you know the process it is important to understand that the parasite doesn't harm the snail or slug by any means. The critter just unknowingly slithers around with the parasite, and living its life with the parasite living in it, and once an animal or even a human eats it, they get sick from a critter that looks completely Harmless.

How can you prevent your GALS from getting this disease?

You can also put out rat poison to get rid of the rats, or make sure that your enclosure is very secure, and rat droppings cannot be laid inside of it. Also, make sure that if you see rat droppings, remove them immediately, as your dog or other household pets can also catch rat round lung worm.

If you need to touch a snail with this disease, in order to isolate them from the rest of the group for example, make sure you wash your hands every time you touch your snail. You can also buy surgical gloves from amazon to prevent coming into contact with a diseased snail.

1. The Importance of Clean Hands

Pet snails are easy to care for, and they are fun to look at, and enjoy in the home that you provide for them. However, I cannot stress enough to you the importance of clean hands. Snails might not just carry the rat around lung worm, but they also carry salmonella, and other bacteria and germs, that the human body is not used to fighting off. The good news is that not all snails and slugs carry the rat around lungworm, as you learned from the previous chapters, but they all do carry salmonella. I'm not trying to scare you away from snails and slugs by telling you that they carry salmonella, and if it makes you feel any better, almost all animals carry salmonella even common pets such as dogs, and birds. Reptiles, amphibians, insects, and all critters that crawl on the dirt carry salmonella. Some people freak out once they learn that the pet they just bought from the pet store carries salmonella, but what they fail to understand is that salmonella comes from the soil or what you would call dirt. The critters crawl into the ground and they contract salmonella, and once they have salmonella their offspring the also contract salmonella from their parents, and from the dirt.

While people are standing around saying "don't touch any critters because they carry salmonella." What about the mud pies that their children make with their friend's next door? The mud that their kids play in has salmonella too. In fact, dirt is one of the main ways that spreads salmonella. Is salmonella a common bacteria? Absolutely! You cannot rid your snail of salmonella completely, but washing your hands thoroughly with antibacterial wash every time you touch the snail will stop you from catching it!

2. Signs of a Sick Snail

The bad news about having a snail as a pet is that they are not like cats and dogs, which make noises, limp, or stop their daily habits when they are sick. This means that it is tough if not impossible to point out an infected snail. One of the most common signs of any sick animal is that they stop eating. The other most common sign that your pet is ill is that it doesn't move around as much as it used to. That is why when you go to a pet shop to buy any animal, the pet shop owners advise you to pick an animal that is moving around a lot of verses an animal that is not moving so much. Unfortunately, when it comes to snails and slugs, you really cannot tell if they, have stopped eating, or have stopped moving around as much because they move in such a slow pace to begin with. Usually, when a snail or slug is sick, you don't find out about it until after you find it dead in its cage. That is just one of the cons of raising slugs. If you do suspect your snail is sick, look for ANY change from normal behavior, and take them to the vet immediately.

If you see a crack in one of your snails shells, that usually means that the snail is not getting enough calcium. If that is the case then you have a few options, you could choose to let that particular snail go, or you can put more opportunities for the snail to get more calcium by adding more rocks, and shells, and even try giving your critters crushed up Tums, and put the snail with the cracked shell right on top of the crushed up Tums that way so he would have first access to the calcium. The third option is to isolate the snail into a different container, so that it could have complete excess to all the calcium you give it.

The option you choose depends on the severity of the shell fracture. If the shell is severely cracked, then it is best to let it go because the opening of the crack is going to give the snail more opportunities to get an illness that could possibly spread to the others.

Conclusion

Giant African Land Snails can make wonderful, entertaining and educational pets for people of all ages. The range of different species and types on offer mean that keeping these snails can start to become a fascinating hobby. They are an excellent choice as a first pet for children or classroom pets due to their slow rate of movement and relatively low maintenance. They can also be observed and studied safely without the need for frequent handling and so, offer an excellent introduction for younger children into the captivating world of nature. I hope this book has given you a better understanding of Giant African Land Snails, in particular the safe and responsible keeping of them as pets.

Published by AAV Publishing 2017